Brenda Lee & Harley

A LOVE STORY
THE TALE OF SLOBBERS BEGINS

WRITTEN AND ILLUSTRATED BY MARI MEEHAN

Copyright © 2020 by Mari Meehan

This book is a work of fiction. The characters, places and events in this story are fictional. Any similarities to real people, places, or events are not intentional and purely the result of coincidence.
Formatting by Self-Publishing Services, LLC

Published by Yellow Snow Publishing
ISBN 978-1-7336199-4-3
Library of Congress Control Number: 2021902980

All rights reserved. No part of this book may be reproduced, scanned, redistributed or transmitted in any form or by any means, print, electronic, mechanical, photocopying, recording, or otherwise, without prior written permission of the author.

Dedication

This book is dedicated to Tammy Evans and Hannah Marshall for graciously allowing me to pattern Slobbers parents, Brenda Lee and Harley, after...well, Brenda Lee and Harley.

Very special thanks to Kayla Jenkins, Creative Writing instructor at Nixyaawii Community School, a charter school that is part of the Confederated Tribes of the Umatilla Indian Reservation, and her students Kenzie Kiona, Maxwell Jean Madden, and Nizhoni Toledo for their editorial contributions.

...and of course to all the Saints who have left us, are with us, and are to come.

Preface

I've long thought I'd like my creation of Slobbers to be the Saint who lives forever for all those who have loved and lost their own.

Slobbers is just that to me, combining the characteristics of the four Saints I had the privilege of living with for most of my adult life, which has been considerable.

In discussing our lost boys with a friend, we decided, jokingly, that her dog, Harley, should become Slobbers' dad in a future story.

Not long after, I found the perfect lady for him. Brenda Lee, who, too, had recently crossed that confounded Rainbow Bridge. I asked her human mom if she'd mind if I patterned Slobbers mom after Brenda Lee and she graciously agreed.

I began doing some social media posts about the two. How they met. How the romance developed. Soon followers were asking for a book. And here we are.

The humans are total figments of my imagination, but the Saints? Well, I think there is a bit of every Saint who has ever graced this earth in each of them.

For this, I make no apologies.

Prologue

Family. It's the most important thing in the world whether you're a dog, like me, living with humans or humans just living with each other.

I found that out living with the White kids, Bud and Sis, and hangin' with their best friends. I came to understand early on about rules and consequences for not obeying them. Fear. Courage and pride. Communication. Love, respect and expectations and how all that blends together and makes life the adventure that it is.

It was a lot for me to absorb, not yet a year old. It got me to thinking about my own Mom and Dad. We puppies only get to hang with our parents for maybe two or three months before we're shuttled off to live with humans. Man, we miss so much!

After my sisters were adopted and my twin and I were awaiting what would become of us, we spent a lot of time listening while Mom and Dad instilled in us just what it was to be a Saint Bernard and what was expected of us, by telling us their own story.

I'm repeating the story to you as best I can. I love all my families, and I've had a few. In learning about all of us, who we are and how we understand ourselves, I'm hoping you come to appreciate why we are, in fact, Saints.

Slobbers

Brenda Lee & Harley
A Love Story

The countryside around Serenity, Calamity and Chaos was dotted with small farms and cottages for those who preferred not to live in the villages.

One of the families, back a bit in time, had a Saint Bernard. His name was Harley. He had swagger and was as macho as the bike that was his namesake. His favorite thing in the world was riding with his dad in the family pickup, his ears and jowls flapping, his slobber flying in the wind.

Harley had a good, if lonely, life. His dad worked in construction and always took Harley to wherever he was working so Harley didn't have to spend long days alone. His mom also worked, so she, too, was never home during the day.

When they were all

together, in the evenings after dinner, both his mom and dad were tired and wanted to do little more than relax and watch television. His walks were most often short. The only time they paid much attention to him was on weekends, which was great, but they never lasted long enough.

Though he knew he was dearly loved, Harley wished he had a companion with whom he could romp and play. He was, after all, a very young Saint Bernard with boundless energy and no way to get rid of it. It made him sad and frustrated and at a loss as to what to do. Television bored him so he spent most evenings curled up by himself wishing his people would get him a companion and looking forward to the next morning when he'd at least get a ride in the pick-up.

One day his dad began a new job, and Harley was really excited. He knew he'd get to see some new scenery. Boy, did he!

All of a sudden there she was! The most beautiful girl he had ever seen, and she was a Saint Bernard. She was gorgeous and all dressed up in summer finery. Human type clothes? What was that about? A bonnet! Leggings! Even flip flops. And slobber. Boy, oh boy, did she have slobber. The sign of a true Saint.

"Was that a smile?" He wondered as they whizzed past.

When they got home that evening his dad mentioned to his mom that Harley had been acting strange all day. Concerned, she went to the yard to check on him and found him lying flat on his back with a paw over his heart. He hadn't touched his dinner, he just lay there. She could see his heart thumping under his paw.

She worried he might be sick.

Well, he was. Love sick. He was totally, head over heels in love.

Harley's time at the construction site wasn't much different from when he was home. While at first he kept busy exploring the new work site, it soon became all too familiar, and while the men worked, he had nothing to do but lounge around. Sometimes they played with him a bit during their lunch break, but it wasn't much. He was restless.

One day, he worried his imagination was playing tricks on him because his lady love hadn't been in her yard. He decided to backtrack the route to work and find the picket fence and mailbox where he was sure he had seen her.

There she was! What? Eating peas straight from the vine? Peas? Wow, he thought. What a gal. She has everything. Plenty of slobber, impeccable vine manners and a lot of meat on her bones. He was sure that hadn't come from eating peas, however. She made him think of a nice, juicy pork chop. Pork chop and peas. What a combo. It made him hungry.

With that he headed back to his dad's work site before he was missed. Plus, he suddenly felt very shy and not at all sure how best to approach her. That can happen when you're in love!

The next day Harley left the work site as soon as he could see his dad was busy and wouldn't notice. When he got to the picket fence, he took a deep breath and approached the lady. What was she studying so intently? A bug? Harley liked bugs, too, though he wasn't so sure about peas. Maybe, he thought, this could possibly work. They did seem to have some things in common.

"Hi, I'm...I'm Harley," he stammered.

"Brenda Lee." She gave him a sassy smile.

"You're beautiful."

"You're pretty okay yourself," she told him as she sniffed at the bug.

"May...may I come by tomorrow night when we might have some time?" he asked shyly. "I'm pretty sure I can get out."

She flicked the bug toward him. "Please do."

His heart soared.

Harley, being a clever guy, made sure the gate wasn't locked behind them when he and his dad got home from work. Luckily, his mom and dad went shopping after dinner, leaving him time to put his plan into action.

He found his barrel, which was kept in the pantry. He had long ago taught himself how to open doors. He rustled around in the kitchen until he found a funnel. He managed to grab hold of the stopper in his barrel and the cork of the brandy bottle, removed them, and ever so carefully filled his barrel. He then hid the barrel in the shrubs beside the gate.

Once his mom and dad had gone to bed for the night, Harley took off toward the picket fence, the barrel dangling from his mouth by its strap. He did his best not to slobber too much.

Brenda Lee was nowhere to be seen when he arrived, but he knew instinctively she would appear when she was ready. He set the barrel on the ground, then nosed around until he found a couple of dandelions with nice long stems. He nipped the flowers off, pulled the plug out of his barrel, and put the stems in. Perfect. Straws.

Then Brenda Lee appeared, as always, all dressed up. This time she wore a tiara, glittery leggings, and pearls. She looked spectacular!

"I can tell you're curious," Brenda Lee murmured between slurps of fine brandy. "You see, I'm a therapy dog, and when the people in the home have parties, I dress for the occasion. It seems to make them happy, and that makes me happy. It's what I'm supposed to do." She studied him for a moment. "You're so sweet. I think you could be a therapy dog, too."

Harley had found the companion of his dreams, and he was beside himself with joy. Every day after the men's lunch break, he went to visit Brenda Lee. Even if she wasn't there, he'd wait. Then he'd hurry back to the construction site just before his dad finished up for the day.

One day, Harley lost track of time, and his dad was frantic. "He leaves every day after lunch. Goes the same way you come," the men told him. "What's the big deal?"

Jumping into his pickup, he retraced their route and sure enough, there was Harley, behind the picket fence, snuggled up with Brenda Lee, totally unaware of the time.

Brenda Lee's mom appeared to see who was visiting. "Is this your dog?" she asked Harley's dad.

"He is. I'm so sorry. I'm working down the road a ways and I guess he wandered off. I hope he didn't cause any trouble."

"Not at all. We enjoy having him around. He comes every day, whether we're here or not. He's here when we get home. What's his name?"

"Harley. His name is Harley."

"Well, why don't you drop him off in the mornings and pick him up when you finish work? Brenda Lee enjoys his company, and he's no trouble at all. Brenda Lee, you know, is a therapy dog. Maybe Harley would like to be one, too."

Harley's dad looked at him. "I'm sure he'd love it, but I don't have the time to train him. Nor the money…" his voice trailed off.

"Don't worry," Brenda Lee's mom assured him. "We'll take care of it."

Harley and Brenda Lee looked at each other in wonder. It was like her mom had read their minds.

The very next day, Brenda Lee's mom began putting Harley through the paces to see if he had the makings of a therapy dog. He was a natural. Of course, with Brenda Lee by his side to encourage him and give him pointers, it was a slam dunk.

Harley soon made his debut at the memory care home. The first few days, he just followed Brenda Lee around, observing. She was wonderful; gentle, loving, and totally non-judgmental. You could even say Saintly.

The ladies really seemed to be drawn to her and she to them though, Harley thought, it might be the Ritz crackers they fed her. Especially the ones smeared with butter or cream cheese and maybe a slice or two of meat on them. That, he reasoned, might be why she reminded him of a nice, succulent pork chop. She had a lot of meat on her bones!

One pair of ladies were of particular interest to Brenda Lee, and Harley found them curious. Their names were Mable and Lorraine. Every day, without fail, they sat at the same table. Lorraine would pat Brenda Lee on the head and give her some crackers. Mable would say, "Why, what a pretty doggy. I wonder who she belongs to."

Then Lorraine would say, "Mable, she's here all the time. She comes to visit."

"What's her name?" Mable would ask.

"Brenda Lee," Lorraine would sigh.

The routine never changed until one day Mable wasn't at the table.

"Where's Mable?" Brenda Lee's mom asked Lorraine.

Lorraine shrugged and said nothing, refusing to look up. Brenda Lee knew where she would be.

Mable was in her room, in bed, looking very wan. Brenda Lee rested her chin on the side of the bed then licked her cheek. Mable opened her eyes and looked at her.

"Why aren't you a pretty doggy," she whispered. "Did you come to visit me?" She rolled over on her side making just enough room for Brenda Lee to crawl up on the bed with her. She snuggled her head into Mable's shoulder and gently laid her paw across her.

That's how they were when the nurse arrived. She patted Brenda Lee's head, then checked Mable's pulse. "She's gone," the attendant whispered.

Brenda Lee looked up at her for a minute, then licked Mable's cheek one last time before she slid back to the floor.

Brenda Lee's mom had come into the room and looked questioningly at the nurse.

"She has no family." The nurse had a tear in her eye as she spoke. "Brenda Lee seemed to know and always paid special attention to her. At least she passed knowing she was loved. By a pretty doggy."

Harley found his own people of interest. Two elderly gentlemen, Fred and Earl, rarely mingled with the others. They always sat together but were never seen chatting. They just sat. Both always wore their service medals and veterans caps. Sometimes they'd munch on a hot dog or a

hamburger. Fred always saved a bite for Harley. Earl never did.

Earl, the younger of the two, would then hoist himself out of his chair, collect his cane, and tell Harley they needed to "march." And so they would. Through the corridors and into the yard, if the weather was good, then back to where Fred would still be sitting.

Veterans Day came. Brenda Lee dressed up like a World War II WAC and Harley as an army sergeant. They did their work together that day because there were several veterans, like Fred and Earl, plus many others who had lost loved ones in the wars. There had been a small but special ceremony. Harley dutifully marched with Earl, as always, and Brenda Lee accompanied them. When they got back to where Fred was usually sitting, they found him standing at full attention. He saluted as Harley approached.

"Soldier," he rasped, "You deserve a medal for putting up with that old codger. Let's go get us a hot dog." And so they did.

That was the way it was in the home. Harley and Brenda Lee brought a light to eyes that often saw none. They made friends and they lost friends, and it brought them close.

Winter descended. Construction work ended, and Harley's dad took to plowing snow to help make ends meet. He could no longer drop Harley off at Brenda Lee's house every morning.

Brenda Lee's mom knew how much Harley was missed at the home, and she also knew his parents had great difficulty having him as a responsibility. She and her husband talked it over and decided to offer to adopt Harley into their own family. They had come to love him as much as Brenda Lee did.

After a lot of heartfelt soul searching, for they dearly loved him, Harley's dad and mom decided to do what everyone thought was best for Harley. They agreed between themselves it had been a mistake to get him just because he was such a cuddly, cute puppy. Trying to keep him would just be another mistake. It was agreed they could visit whenever they wanted.

Harley and Brenda Lee were very people savvy by this time and understood a sacrifice had been made. Harley had mixed emotions, for he loved his dad and mom, but he also loved Brenda Lee's dad and mom. He and Brenda Lee knew, too, it was best for all concerned. They really loved each other, and they belonged together.

Brenda Lee's and Harley's lives were bright and full and fun until winter decided to unleash its fury. It snowed day after day. It just kept coming and piled up deeper and deeper. There were many days their mom couldn't get them to the home. The weather and the roads were just too dangerous. To make matters worse, a huge blizzard was forecast.

One especially bad day, Brenda Lee's mom received a call from the home asking if she could lend a hand. Most of the staff and volunteers were snowed in. Wisely, she decided to leave the dogs at home.

Hours later, Brenda Lee and Harley were getting frantic. Their people hadn't returned. They began to worry. They were also very hungry. Together they rummaged around the counter tops and found a box of Brenda Lee's beloved Ritz crackers. Harley managed to get the refrigerator door open, where they found a couple of packages of hot dogs. They hoped it would be enough to tide them over.

Still later, no one had come home. "I think," Brenda Lee said, "We need to go look for them."

"But where?" Harley asked.

"The home would be a good place to start. Maybe Dad met her there."

Harley reluctantly agreed.

Not knowing what to expect, they found a grocery bag and stuffed it with what was left of the hot dogs and

crackers and Harley's brandy barrel.

Harley tried the doggy door. It had been snowed in for days, but he pushed and pushed until it opened. He pushed the bag through with no trouble. Brenda Lee was a different matter. Too many Ritz crackers, Harley chuckled to himself as he planted his head firmly against Brenda Lee's behind and pushed and pushed until she popped through.

The weather was brutal. The wind howled, and the snow swirled around them.

"Wow," Harley muttered. "You really think this is a good idea?"

"We have to find them!" Brenda Lee insisted.

Into the night they went, but to where they weren't sure. There were no lights nor scents to follow. They couldn't see any landmarks, so they just chose a direction and headed off.

Heads down against the wind, they plodded and pushed through the blizzard all night. When dawn finally broke they saw nothing but a white expanse. What few buildings they could see were far away and nearly buried. They didn't recognize anything. To make matters worse, it was still snowing hard.

"We better find some shelter," Harley said, "and eat something. We need our strength."

They looked around but saw nothing. They were crestfallen, exhausted, and lost.

Suddenly Harley saw a dark shape that seemed to be moving. It looked like a man, though he was so caked in ice and snow it was hard to tell. It looked like he was carrying something. It was bawling its head off and sounded just like a calf. A man with a calf out in this? Harley and Brenda looked at each other in wonder.

The man had seen them, too. He was collapsed in a heap in front of them, clinging to the calf who was still bawling like a baby. Well, it was a baby.

"Where….w…w…w…where did you two come from?" His teeth were chattering so hard, Harley and Brenda Lee could hardly understand him. Harley dropped the bag in front of him, and Brenda Lee went to the calf and began licking ice and snow off its face.

The man couldn't believe his eyes. He took the brandy keg in his shaking hands and took himself a healthy swig. "Food? Food? Where did you get food?" He shared a hot dog and some crackers with his calf then returned the food to the bag. "Can…can you help me break a path?" He gasped and pointed the direction. Harley picked up the bag, then shoulder to shoulder Harley and Brenda Lee forged ahead.

After what seemed forever, they came upon a cottage behind an outcropping of rocks that had been sheltered from the drifting. All three of them collapsed against the door, the man still clasping the calf against his chest. Harley and Brenda Lee barked as loud as they could, the man pounded with all his might, and the calf continued to bawl, all hoping someone inside would hear. Finally, a woman opened the door.

"Johan!" she cried. "I was so worried, so worried! Oh, my goodness, you found Dinky. Thank goodness! Whatever happened?"

With the help of Harley and Brenda Lee, she got them all into the warmth of the cottage. Frantically, she tore the icy clothes from Johan, gathered some blankets, wrapped him snugly, and settled him in front of the fire. When she turned her attention to Harley and Brenda Lee, she found them both licking ice off the bewildered calf. She toweled them off then spread out what was left of the crackers and hot dogs. There was little left, but it was welcome. They were exhausted and starving from their efforts.

When Johan was able to speak without his teeth chattering, he explained how Brenda Lee and Harley had found him and the calf. It was a miracle. That chance meeting had saved all their lives.

When the snow finally stopped and the wind died down, no one was thinking they were in a winter wonderland. When the sun hit the snow, it was blinding, and the cold remained unbearable for days. Johan had been able to create a shelter for the calf that kept him warm and unearthed enough hay from his collapsed hay barn to keep him fed. Brenda Lee and Harley were allowed to cozy together in front of the fire.

Johan recovered quickly and doted on Harley and Brenda Lee.

"I wonder who they belong to," his wife, Maria, wondered out loud. "No one lives near, and I've never seen Saint Bernards around this area. And this one, she's just so cute with her bow and leggings." She had made Brenda Lee some clean bows and leggings. "My, they truly are Saints, aren't they?"

"Ya. They are indeed, they are indeed," Johan agreed.

The snow remained for weeks. Harley and Brenda Lee enjoyed being with these new people. They were kept dry, warm, and fed. They never stopped worrying about their other people, though. What had happened to them? Were they safe? Would they ever see them again?

Time passed, and the weather finally began to warm. The snow melted enough so that Johan could go outside and survey the damage the storm left behind. It was severe. His barn and storage sheds had collapsed under the weight of the snow; his equipment was ruined, too. He and Maria had sunk everything they had into their little farm, and now all looked to be lost. Johan wasn't sure he'd even be able to sell what was left for scrap. How was he ever going to provide for himself and Maria, what's more two huge dogs and Maria's pet, the calf named Dinky? Because that's what he was. Dinky. She had gotten him from a nearby farmer who said he wasn't up to standard for the herd and was going to kill him. Maria would have none of it. Johan couldn't understand why she felt as she did. What were they going to do with a male calf as it grew up? He knew she'd never let him have it killed for beef. He was destined to become a 2000 pound pet. He'd require a lot of hay.

Learning Dinky's story from conversations, Maria became Harley and Brenda Lee's very favorite person. She wouldn't let the calf be killed just because he wasn't perfect. They weren't sure why that mattered, but they knew if Maria hadn't stepped in, Dinky would no longer be. How great was it for her to do that? Very.

Harley, being very smart, came up with an idea for making Dinky more acceptable to Johan. He'd train him to be a watch cow just like Brenda Lee taught had taught him to be a therapy dog. Every home needed to be protected. Harley figured it didn't matter who did the protecting.

In time, Johan and Maria decided they should put a notice in their paper about having found two lost Saint Bernards. The closest town was Chaos. Brenda Lee and Harley's people lived closer to Calamity. Serenity was in between. Though they, too, put ads in their paper looking for their dogs, neither was seen by the right people.

Having a new family wasn't a problem for Harley since he'd been through it before, but he worried about Brenda Lee. She seemed to be losing interest in everything. She was usually full of vim and vigor, but now all she wanted to do was lounge around the house with Maria. Was she missing her Ritz crackers? Was she frightened of something or angry with him about anything?

One night he snuggled extra close to her and hesitantly asked what the trouble was.

"Nothing, no trouble," she said softly. "It's…it's just that you're going to be… a father."

"Me?" Harley was so excited he let out an arf. He could barely contain himself. "Me? A dad?"

She nuzzled him affectionately. "But don't get too excited," she cautioned. "Humans always find new homes for our kids, our puppies."

"I'm not so sure I like that," Harley grumbled."We can't raise our own kids?"

"Well, that's the way people are. We get to enjoy them for maybe three months, then off they go," Brenda Lee sounded sad and looked away.

"Hmmmph." Harley decided he needed to think about that. Then he remembered, that was about the age he was when he went to his first family. They were good to him, but they should never have gotten him. Brenda Lee's family was totally different. They spent all the time they could with Brenda Lee and Harley. Funny, he never thought about his mom and dad. Was that part of the plan? You were never together long enough to form a bond? That didn't make him feel any better. The bond he and Brenda Lee had was so wonderful. He reveled in it and knew she did, too. He thought he'd liked to have the chance to form the same bond with his kids.

Soon, Harley and Brenda Lee noticed their portions of food were getting smaller. Harley gave most of his to Brenda Lee so she would stay strong. He was strong and

tough and could do with a bit less. They noticed the meals Maria served she and Johan were also getting smaller.

Brenda Lee was staying in the house more and more, but Harley accompanied Johan when he slogged through his fields. He also spent a lot of time getting acquainted with Dinky. He never had a cow for a friend, and not knowing what to talk about, he put his plan into action and taught him about being a watch cow. That, he figured, would give Maria and Johan ample protection should he and Brenda Lee ever have to move on.

The two had fun together. Harley taught Dinky how to crouch and even emit a cow version of a growl.

One day he noticed some little nubbins on Dinky's head and nudged Johan until he looked.

"Those," Johan told him, "are the beginnings of horns. That's why the little guy is not up to standard. That's why our neighbor was going to kill him. His kind of cow isn't supposed to have horns."

Why isn't a cow supposed to have horns? Harley wondered, thinking of the western movies he sometimes watched with his former people. Those cows had horns. Oh well, he figured, horns would sure add to Dinky's ability to be a watch cow.

Johan had plenty of problems and always returned to the cottage depressed. He knew he wouldn't be able to get a crop in without his equipment. What would he do? He knew nothing other than farming.

One morning the sun finally peeked through the leaden clouds bringing some cheer to the cottage. Maria, bringing

them their breakfast, found Harley standing over Brenda Lee, looking as proud as he could be.

"Oh, my!" Maria clapped her hand over her mouth. "Oh my, oh my! Come look, Johan! We have a family!"

"What? What are you talking about?"

He joined Maria where Harley and Brenda Lee always slept. There she was, nursing five brand new babies.

"Oh, my, oh, my," They both repeated over and over. "What are we going to do now?"

"We'll figure it out, Johan. Look at them. They are so tiny and helpless. We'll figure it out."

As time passed, the puppies grew into fluff balls. Maria was beside herself with joy at having them around. Johan wasn't quite so enthused because he had to dip into what had been untouchable funds in order to keep all of them fed, plus he had to buy hay for Dinky. He knew, as spring approached, he was going to have to look for a job in order to make ends meet.

"You know," he said to Maria, "we're not going to be able to keep both the puppies and their parents and Dinky."

Maria looked at him with tears in her eyes. "I know," she said, "I know."

"Maybe we should go to town soon, with the puppies, and sell them to people we think would take good care of them. That would give us a little money."

Maria nodded, knowing it was something that had to be done. "I just hope we're good judges of character," she whispered.

"Ya, me too. I'm attached to them, too, you know." Johan put his arm around his wife and held her as she wept. "I've even grown fond of that calf of yours."

Maria smiled at that.

Harley and Brenda Lee kept the puppies close and explained to them what they hoped would come next in their young lives.

Johan and Maria got permission from the grocery to sit in front with the puppies. People fell in love with them, as people do with Saint Bernard puppies.

"Oh, they are soooo cute," one wife said to her husband. "Couldn't we? Please?"

"No," he said softly. "You know what happened last time we had a dog. With both of us working, it's just not possible. You know that."

She nodded, not wanting to move away from the box. "I know," she said, softly. "I know. I think about Harley a lot, though, and how much I miss him."

Others came by, too. Many oohed and aahed and moved on. Saint Bernards? They get too big. They slobber too much. Too much to deal with.

Just before the day was over, one more couple came by and looked in the box. The women lifted the chin of each of the girls and studied their faces intently. "Look at these faces," she exclaimed to her husband. "They remind me of both Harley and Brenda Lee!"

"But the other two don't look anything like either of them," he chuckled. "I think you'd see Harley and Brenda Lee in any litter of Saints."

"Let's take the girls," the wife said. "The home really misses having therapy dogs."

"What about the boys?" Her husband asked.

"They be identical twins," Johan offered. "Look at their markings."

"They should stay together," the wife said, "and we can't take on all five. But we will take the girls. I'm sure you'll find a good home for the little guys, too."

The next two weekends, Maria and Johan took the twin boys to different locations, hoping someone would give them a home. Alas, no one was willing. That evening, over dinner, Johan brought up the subject he didn't want to address. "You know, Maria, we can't keep all four of the dogs. I'm not finding work and our funds are running out."

"I know, I know," she said. "I've been giving it a lot of thought, too. I don't like the alternative."

"Nor do I, but I see no other way."

"The shelter."

Johan nodded, not wanting to meet her eyes.

"Which of them?" Tears were streaming down her cheeks.

"I think the puppies would have a better chance than the adults," Johan said softly. "Especially a male and an un-fixed female. I don't have the heart to sell them, or even give them away, separately. Besides, they're the ones who saved my life."

Maria nodded.

Brenda Lee and Harley spent all the time they could with their boys, trying to squeeze in a lifetime. They told them everything about themselves, their purpose in life, and finally, implored upon them to live the legacy of the Saint Bernard.

Then the day came. Leaving Maria home, Johan gathered up the twins and took the all too short drive to the shelter.

You may think this is where the story ends, but no, it isn't. It's where the tale of Slobbers begins…

About the Author

Mari Meehan spent her career as a public relations professional and her personal life as a lover of Saint Bernards.

Her retirement years brought a stint as a blogger then, encouraged by friends, she turned her attention to writing a story she had long harbored in her imagination.

The original concept of her first book, Slobbers and Slime, was to be a spoof of monster movies but soon morphed into an adventure/mystery for children with a somewhat bemused Saint Bernard puppy as the hero.

The more she wrote, the more the story evolved and soon caught the attention of the Saint Bernard community on social media.

The narrative was paused for a prequel to explain how Slobbers, the hero, became a shelter dog. That being completed, the story shall continue with the cast of familiar characters and many new ones as long as her imagination remains.

More can be found at slobbersandslime.com

Slobbers and Slime

CHAPTER 1

Clank! Click!

"Hoooooowl! Let me out of here! Where's my brother?" I'm shouting in my loudest most very biggest puppy voice.

"Shhhhh little fella. You'll be okay." Some guy with an 'Animal Shelter Staff' tag on his shirt says, scratching my ears which I usually like but not from him. "Your brother is right here too."

Who the heck are you? Oh, man! My twin brother and I were taken from Mom and brought to this place called a shelter and put in...in cages! With bars! Big, thick, heavy bars! It's just awful. I don't wanna be here. I want my Mom!

I hear a "woof" behind me. Yippee! I know that voice. I turn to look around and there is my brother. Thank goodness. We've always been together. I don't want to lose him too.

Mom's people told her no one wanted us and they couldn't keep us because we are Saint Bernards. Whimper. What does being a Saint Bernard have to do with anything? Heck, there were five of us and all the girls went to new homes. Why did we boys end up here?

Oh no! Someone comes and picks up my brother and takes him away. He's howling something awful. Bro? Bro? Noooo! Now I'm all alone. I'm scared. Where did they take him? Will he be back? Will I ever see him again? Hoooowll!

We dogs understand a lot. We just can't talk like people do. Cages with bars are scary and the floors are hard and cold. The little crates they stick us in when we're born are bad enough, but this is just awful.

Click. C-r-e-a-k.

Oh no! Someone new. A man's picking me up. And he's got a lady with him. Who are these people? What are they going to do with me? Where's my brother?

They're patting my head and tickling my tummy and are smiling and laughing. They're happy. I like happy. All puppies like happy. I think they like me. The lady holding me smells nice. Whoa! Now we're leaving the building. Where are we going?

Quick as a wink, I find myself in the back of a car. I sniff the floor around me and find crumbs and crumpled paper and bits of dirt and people smells not of the people in the front seat. I've never seen or smelled stuff like this before. I'm learning my nose tells me a lot. We ride for a short time. The people are laughing about how their kids have been begging for a puppy and what a surprise I'll be. Especially since I'll grow up to be a really big dog which is what they want. One they can wrestle with and run and play with. Kids. That must be who all this stuff and new smells come from.

The car stops. They pick me up again and set me down on some nice green grass. It smells like the fresh mowed grass we romped on before we were sent off to that shelter place. I didn't like the smell of that place. I do like the smell of this place. I cock my head and look around. Wow! This is pretty darn nice. I see a house and beautiful flowers and lots of trees. You wonder how I know about grass and houses and crumbs and stuff like that? I'm three months old ya know. I'm no dummy.

The people from the car call out, "Bud, Sis! Where are you? We've got a surprise for you. Deon and Lin, come on along too."

Slobbers & Sleuths

SLOBBERS

"No! Noooo. He's dead!" Bud's voice is quivering. He's staring wide-eyed at the big man standing beside him. "Cole Black is supposed to be dead!"

All of our emotions are crackling like the fire in front of us. What just happened? This man I've lived with since growing too big to live with Bud's family has just revealed he's the "lost boy," Cole Black, who disappeared from the Village of Serenity years ago.

People think he is dead because no sign of him has ever been found. Or so we all thought. But here he is. Very much alive.

Cole furrows his brow and stares at Bud long and hard. Bud takes a step backward. Bro and I shift ourselves from lethargic watching to full alert.

"He is... I am not dead. You can see I'm not." His voice is low and very quiet. "The story you've heard is no more true than the ones that say I took growth hormones so I could play football."

"But...but why?" Bud looks confused, his mouth drooping at the corners.

Bro and I are confused, too. I call him Bro 'cause he's my twin brother, but other than the four of us together now, everyone thinks he's me—Slobbers— and calls him that. Ya see, we swapped places when I got too big to live with Bud and the rest of my family, and he was livin' with Cole. Bro just didn't get into to that growth stuff that made me, the snails, and Cole turn into giants. Man, you talk about confusing. I guess this is why what happened to Cole is a big mystery.

"Why...why didn't you tell me? I thought you trusted me," Bud stammers. "Why didn't you at least tell your parents? How could you let them think you're dead?"

"You have no idea what the real story is." Cole's voice is still very quiet, but it has a bit of an edge to it. He pulls up his collar and pokes at the dwindling fire with a stick. "I hope you'll give me a chance to explain before you go jumping to any more conclusions."

"Explain? You've never explained anything to me. Like why you live like...like this! Like a hermit." Bud waves his arm at the fire and the woods around us. "How can you be so good and kind and smart and yet be..."

"And yet be what?"

"I dunno. So secretive."

"Secretive? You've never asked me anything. Ever.

And I'm not as secretive as you seem to think." Cole studies Bud, then shrugs his shoulders. His voice returns to normal.

Made in the USA
Monee, IL
13 July 2022